REMEMBER HER™

The moment a woman stops searching for power and realizes she already is it.

Kendra Tamika

Remember Her Publishing

Published by Remember Her Publishing
ISBN: 979-8-9954705-0-2
LCCN: 2026909898
First Edition
Printed in the United States of America

www.kendratamika.com
www.rememberherpublishing.com

Dedication

For my daughter, who came into this world fighting before she ever took her first breath.
You taught me strength before I understood what it meant.

And For every woman who has ever forgotten herself while trying to love everyone else.

May this book help you remember.

Table of Contents

This book is not one thing.

It is a memoir and a mirror. It is my story and an invitation for you to look more honestly at your own. It is personal and it is practical because I have never believed that healing happens in theory alone. It happens in the quiet moments when you finally tell yourself the truth.
When I started writing Remember Her, I was not sure what shape it would take. What I knew was this: there were things I had lived through that I wish someone had handed me a book about. Not a book that told me what to do. But a book that made me feel less alone in what I was already feeling.

That is what I tried to write for you.

Each chapter moves through a different season of my journey from the moment I first realized I had lost myself, through the years of carrying more than I was ever meant to carry, through the breaking point, the rebuilding, and finally the reclaiming. You may recognize yourself in some of these seasons. You may have already survived others. You may be standing in the middle of one right now.

Wherever you are, you are welcome here.

At the end of each chapter you will find a section called Remember Her Reflection. These are not homework assignments. They are invitations. Questions designed to help you turn the page inward to sit with your own story the way I had to learn to sit with mine. Take your time with them. Write your answers down if that feels right. Or simply let the questions live in you for a while. There is no wrong way to remember yourself.

This book can be read straight through or one chapter at a time. You can return to the chapters that speak to your current season. You can underline the lines that feel like they were written for you because in many ways, they were.

My only request is this.

Read it honestly. Let it reach the places you have been protecting. And when something inside you stirs that quiet voice that has been waiting for you to finally listen do not push it down this time.

That voice is the whole reason I wrote this book.
She has been trying to reach you for a long time.

With love, Kendra Tamika

You Didn't Lose Yourself. You Forgot Her.

Somewhere along the way, a lot of women disappear.

Not in dramatic ways. Not overnight.

It happens slowly. Quietly. Respectably.

You become the supportive partner. The responsible daughter. The dependable employee. The mother who holds everything together. You become the woman everyone can count on.

And one day you wake up and realize something unsettling.

Everyone else knows exactly who you are supposed to be.

Except you.

This book is not about becoming someone new.

It is about remembering the woman you were before the world told you who you needed to be.

Because the truth is, most women do not lose themselves in one moment. They lose themselves in a thousand small decisions. A thousand quiet compromises. A thousand times choosing peace over truth.

And if you are honest, you have probably felt it before.

That quiet voice inside you that whispers: This is not the life I imagined.

For some women the awakening comes through heartbreak. For others it comes through motherhood, burnout, loss, or simply waking up one morning and realizing the life they built does not feel like it belongs to them anymore.

For me, it began in a hospital bed.

Before the marriage. Before the divorce. Before I understood what it meant to choose myself.

That was the moment I first realized something inside me had disappeared.

I just did not trust myself enough to listen.

And if you are holding this book, there is a chance you know that feeling too.

This book is for the woman who feels like she has spent years being strong for everyone else. The woman who has survived things she rarely talks about. The woman who sometimes wonders when it will finally be her turn.

You do not need permission to reclaim your life. You do not need approval to become someone new. And you definitely do not need anyone's blessing to step into your power.

You only need one thing.

To remember her.

The woman you were before the world convinced you to forget.

CHAPTER ONE

The Day I Realized I Was Gone

Before I was a patient, I was a baker.

Before I was on bed rest, I was building something. Before the hospital became my world, I had a world. I had a business I was pouring myself into sculpted cakes, dessert tables, events all around Dallas. I was becoming known. People were starting to say my name when they talked about cakes in that city, and my banana pudding the one that would later become my whole second act was just starting to get attention. I had done some print modeling. Won a couple of contests. I was working at Raytheon, which sounds like it does not fit with the cakes and the modeling, but that was who I was. A woman with multiple dimensions, multiple dreams, all of them running at the same time.
And then I lost the Raytheon job.
Which sounds like a blow. And in the moment, it stung. But looking back, I understand it now for what it was a redirect. Because losing that job right before everything happened meant I could be fully present for what was coming. Sometimes the thing that feels like a loss is actually a clearing.
I was in my second trimester when they admitted me.
The diagnosis was early-onset preeclampsia and lupus anticoagulants words I had to learn quickly, the way you learn a new language when you have no choice.

What they meant in plain terms was this: my pregnancy had become dangerous. My body was doing something it was not supposed to do, and the only way to manage it was to keep me still, keep me monitored, keep me in that room until they decided what came next.

The room was actually nicer than I expected.

I remember being almost surprised by it. The walls were a grayish-green not sterile white the way you imagine hospital rooms to be, but something softer, almost like someone had tried to make it feel calm. The bed was centered in the room, which gave it a strange formality, like I was the main event. The TV hung on the wall directly in front of me. The bathroom was to my left, closer to the door. To my right was the couch the kind that pulled out into something like a bed, where visitors could sit or stay.

And above that couch, there were windows.

When the blinds were open and the sun was out, all I could see was sky. I was high enough up that the buildings below were almost an afterthought. On the good days the bright Texas days when the light came in clean and wide that view felt like a promise. Like the world was still out there. Like I was still going to get back to it.

On the rainy days, I tried not to read too much into the gray.

My routine became the rhythm of that room.

They brought me the breakfast menu, the lunch menu, the dinner menu. I ordered my food. I watched television. I did some reading. I could not walk much they did not want me on my feet, did not want my blood pressure climbing. The thrombosis wraps around my legs kept the blood moving so I would not clot. The belly monitor tracked her. The machines beeped.

The nurses came in and out at all hours, including the middle of the night when they would check my pressure, check the readings, remind me to rest which always felt a little cruel, being told to sleep by the very people who kept waking you up.

Sleep was not easy to find in that room.

But the days had their moments of goodness too. My family came my mom, my dad, my sisters. Friends visited. One of my nurses brought me something I did not know I needed: the complete first season of Game of Thrones. The whole collector's set, in a box. She set up the DVD player and I got completely lost in that world. Dragons. Politics. Betrayal. Survival. Looking back, maybe it was not the most ironic show to be watching.

He came to visit too. My boyfriend. The father of the baby I was fighting to keep alive.

He sat in the chair beside me, or on that couch by the windows. He was present enough. There. Physically in the room. But I would learn over time that presence and partnership are not always the same thing.

The day he asked me about California, he was sitting right there.

Right there in that room with me. Not on the phone, not in a text. In person. Looking at me. And he said he wanted to take his other children to visit their grandfather. The grandfather was sick possibly not long for this world, from what he told me and the younger kids had never met him. They were going to Disneyland too. A whole trip. A real experience. And then he looked at me and asked if that would be okay.

My first thought the one I never said out loud was: Why would you even ask me that?

Not because I wanted to stand in the way of his children meeting their grandfather. But because I was in a hospital bed. Because I was carrying his child. Because the doctors had told us, in careful measured language, that this baby may or may not make it. Because I was attached to monitors. Because I could not leave if I wanted to. Because if something happened to her, to me, to both of us he would be on a plane to California.

My real first thought was: Do you even love me? Forget love. Do you even care?

But I did not say that.

Instead I started doing the thing that women do. I started talking myself into a yes.

I thought about his kids. I thought about the grandfather who might not have much time left. I thought about what it would mean for those children to never have that moment, and I told myself I did not want to be the reason. I thought about what he might tell them that they could not go because of me. I thought about how they might feel toward me for that. I thought about all of that before I thought about myself for even one second.

And so I said yes.

He left. And I cried.

Not loudly. Not dramatically. Just the quiet kind of crying you do when you are alone in a hospital room and the person who was just sitting in the chair beside you is now on his way to the airport. The kind of crying that does not ask for anything because there is no one there to ask.

I did not call anyone. I did not reach out to a friend to process it. I just lay there in that grayish-green room with the windows showing me nothing but sky and I cried quietly and then I stopped and I went back to being okay.

That was the first time I chose his comfort over my own pain.

It would not be the last.

The moment I remember most vividly from that entire hospital stay is not the day he asked about California.

It is the day they told me it was time.

My blood pressure had been climbing. They had been watching it, managing it, trying to keep it in a range that was safe for both of us. But one day the nurses came in to check it and something changed in the room. The energy shifted the way it does when professionals stop performing calm and start moving with urgency.

My blood pressure was past stroke level.

I was asymptomatic I did not feel it the way you might expect. No splitting headache, no dizziness, no warning signs that a person without medical training would recognize. My body had been quietly threatening to betray me in a way I could not feel. That is the thing about preeclampsia that nobody tells you it can be invisible right up until it is not.

They said: Prep the OR. Right now.

And I remember lying there thinking: He is not here.

Not as an accusation. Not yet. Just as a fact that landed in my chest like something cold. He was on a trip I had given him permission to take, and I was about to be wheeled into emergency surgery, and he was not here.

I called my mother first. I heard myself tell her what was happening and I heard her voice change that shift a mother's voice makes when she moves from regular person to someone who will be there in whatever amount of time it takes. She left work immediately. She came.

I called him. They were already at the airport or on their way back we had known this possibility existed, that the delivery could happen at any time, so the plan was in place. He made it back. Not for the delivery. But after. He arrived after my mother had already been there, after the surgery was done, after our daughter had already taken her first fragile breaths. He came in and my mother went home.

Our daughter was born tiny.

She was so small that the world she knew for the next ten months would be made of machines and tubes and the hands of nurses and the sound of my voice reading to her through the walls of an incubator. She came into the world fighting before she ever learned what fighting was.

And I sat beside her every day.

And somewhere in those months of sitting beside her, trying to pour my strength into something that small and something that determined, I began to lose track of where she ended and I began. I began to confuse surviving for her with living for myself. I began to believe that my own needs my fear, my loneliness, my grief about what I had seen in my relationship were selfish distractions from the only thing that mattered.

She needed me to be strong.

So I was strong.

And the woman I had been before the baker, the model, the dreamer building her dessert empire, the woman who had looked out hospital windows at pure blue sky and believed the world was still waiting for her she got quieter and quieter.

Until I stopped hearing her at all.

Remember Her Reflection

- When did you first feel that quiet shift the moment something told you things were not right?
- Did you listen to that voice, or did you push it down? What made you choose the way you did?
- Looking back, what were you most afraid of losing if you had listened sooner?
- What would it mean to trust that voice the next time it speaks?

Affirmation

You are not behind. You are not broken. Every moment you stayed was a choice made from love and every moment you choose differently now is also made from love. The difference is that this time, you are including yourself.

Remember Her

The woman who ignored her instincts to keep the peace was not weak. She was doing the best she could with what she knew. Now you know more.

CHAPTER TWO

The Good Woman Trap

Nobody handed me a manual.

There was no sit-down conversation, no formal lesson, no moment where someone looked me in the eyes and said: this is what a good woman does. It was quieter than that. It was absorbed. Watched. Inhaled like air over the course of a childhood until it became so much a part of me that I couldn't tell where the lesson ended and I began.

I learned it from my mother.

She was and still is one of the most remarkable women I have ever known. Strong in the way that certain women are strong, the kind of strength that doesn't announce itself or ask for applause. She pushed past things that would have leveled other people. She made sure her daughters had what they needed. She wanted better for us than what she had growing up, and she sacrificed in ways I am still discovering, still processing, still learning to honor.

But I also watched her endure.

I watched her stay in situations where the men in her life did not treat her the way she deserved. I watched her absorb things verbal things, sometimes physical things and keep going. Keep praying. Keep the family together. Her faith was the architecture of her life, and inside that faith was a belief that God would handle what she could not. That endurance was holy. That staying was strength.

I am not in that place spiritually. I want to be honest about that. I was raised deep inside religion and somewhere along the way, as I got older and saw more and lived more, I found my own relationship with something larger than myself that does not look exactly like what I grew up with. But I am not here to debate faith. I am here to tell you what I saw and what it taught me.

What it taught me was this: a good woman stays. A good woman endures. A good woman does not rock the boat. She prays about it and keeps moving. She handles it quietly and does not make it anyone else's burden. She is strong. She is sacrificial. She puts everyone else first and trusts that somehow, eventually, it will all work out.

I absorbed every single one of those lessons.

And then I carried them straight into my adult relationships and let them cost me everything.

I want to tell you something about being the kid who stayed out of the way.

For a long time I was the second oldest of four children, though our family would eventually grow to nine. I grew up with cousins around, a full loud house, the kind of childhood that had its own ecosystem of personalities and dynamics. And somewhere in all of that I became the kid who was either causing trouble or out of the way entirely. My sister said that about me once, years later, and when she said it I laughed because it was so accurate it was almost funny.

I was also what you might call the weird kid.

I had skin issues growing up. I didn't feel as beautiful as my older sister. I was a tomboy, always hanging around my boy cousins, a little outside of the social rhythms that came naturally to other girls. Kids made their jokes the way kids do. Nothing devastating in isolation just the accumulation of a thousand small moments that taught me I was slightly outside of whatever the acceptable version of a girl was supposed to look like.

So I learned early to either cause a disruption or disappear.

And when I got into relationships my first real relationship at eighteen, because we were not allowed to date before that I chose disappearing. I chose keeping the peace. Not because I had always been that way, but because I think somewhere deep down I had decided that the cost of rocking the boat in love was too high. I had watched what happened when you rocked the boat. I had seen women I loved endure the consequences of demanding too much, needing too much, expecting too much.

So I decided to need less.

I decided to be the woman who made things easy. The woman who understood. The woman who did not add to the pressure. The woman who was, above all else, good.

And that decision that quiet, unexamined decision I made before I even knew I was making it is the one that cost me the most.

I did not start dating until I was eighteen years old.

I want you to sit with that for a moment because I think it matters more than it might seem.

Eighteen years old, having never navigated the territory of romantic love, having watched the women around me handle it in ways that prioritized endurance over honesty, and I walked straight into my first real relationship with no map, no compass, and a heart full of love I did not yet know how to protect.

I was so green. I know that now. I did not know it then.

I put up with things in that first relationship that I had told myself my whole life I would never accept. And I accepted them not because I didn't know better in theory but because in practice, in the actual lived moment, keeping the peace felt more important than honoring what I knew. Love felt like something you proved through endurance. I thought if I was good enough, patient enough, present enough, the relationship would become what I needed it to be.

It was a pattern I would carry forward.

By the time I was in the relationship that would become my marriage, the pattern was deeply established. I was quieter than I had ever been. Not because I had nothing to say I had everything to say but because I had learned to swallow it.

There was the time he took a trip. I will not go into every detail, but what I will tell you is that he came back and I found something in his bag that told me everything I needed to know. Something that had no business being there. And instead of speaking clearly and directly about what I had found, instead of trusting what my eyes were telling me, I went quiet. I told myself he was going through a hard time. I told myself I did not want to add more pressure. I told myself that a good woman stands beside her man in his difficult seasons and does not make things harder.

What I was really telling myself was this: my pain is less important than his comfort.

That is the Good Woman Trap in its purest form. The moment you decide that your discomfort is an inconvenience to someone else's peace.

And it was not just that moment. It was the small daily architecture of that entire relationship. The things I let go. The opinions I kept to myself. The moments I felt disrespected by the other women in his life the mothers of his other children and said nothing because I did not want to be seen as difficult. I never truly felt protected. Not in the way I needed. Not the protection of the heart the sense that someone has you, that someone is thinking about your feelings the way you are always thinking about theirs. That protection was absent for most of that relationship and I made peace with its absence every single day.

I got quieter. I stopped doing the things I loved. I drifted from my friends partly the natural drift that happens when you are deep in a relationship, but partly something more deliberate. Because my friends could see what I could not yet see, and being around them meant being around the truth.

They tried to tell me.

One friend in particular. She would say things about him that he was out here talking to other women, that something wasn't right and I would look at her and say girl, no. We're together. The certainty in my voice. The loyalty I thought I was demonstrating. What I was really doing was choosing him over the people who actually loved me. Over and over again I chose to protect his image over accepting the care of people who were trying to protect me.

I lost those friendships. Not all of them. But enough of them that I noticed the silence.

Our therapist noticed too.

Later in the relationship we went to therapy together, and I remember the therapist looking at me really looking at me and saying something I have never forgotten. She said: I don't even see you in this relationship. She told me that every time I walked away from a difficult conversation I was walking away carrying the other person's weight, absorbing things that did not belong to me. She told me I needed to start saying what needed to be said.

I heard her. And I still couldn't do it.

Because by then the silencing was not just a habit. It was a belief system.

The lie at the center of all of it the one I held onto the longest, the one that did the most damage was this:

If I just love him enough, he will eventually become who I need him to be.

Not that he was a terrible man. I want to be clear about that because this book is not about villainizing anyone. He was a human being with his own story, his own wounds, his own limitations. But I had built an entire internal world around the idea that my love patient enough, quiet enough, sacrificial enough could transform a situation that was not transforming. That if I just stayed. If I just endured. If I just kept being good.

He would eventually protect me. He would eventually provide. He would eventually love me the way my heart needed to be loved.

All I had to do was be there. Be quiet. Be good. Wait.
And in the waiting, in all those years of patient loving, I stopped loving myself.
I am not sure I even walked into that relationship loving myself. I did not know then what self love truly meant. Not in the deep, non-negotiable, I-will-not-accept-less-than-I-deserve way. I knew the word. I did not know the practice.
The Good Woman Trap does not just steal your voice. It steals your standard. It convinces you that wanting more makes you difficult. That needing protection makes you weak. That a woman who truly loves does not keep score, does not make demands, does not draw lines.
What it does not tell you is that a woman without lines has no borders.
And a woman without borders has no self.
That was me. Loving him with everything I had. Giving and giving and giving. Proud of my capacity to give. Calling it strength when it was actually disappearance.
The Good Woman Trap is convincing because it wears the face of virtue. It looks like love. It looks like faith. It looks like the women who raised you doing what they had to do to hold things together.
But somewhere between their survival and your story, the lesson got twisted.
Surviving is not the same as thriving.
Enduring is not the same as choosing.
And staying quiet is not the same as keeping the peace.
It is just keeping someone else comfortable while you slowly come undone.

Remember Her Reflection

- Where did you first learn what a good woman was supposed to look like? Who taught you and did they know they were teaching you?
- What is the lie you have been telling yourself about love the longest? The one that has cost you the most?
- Think of one specific moment where you chose someone else's comfort over your own truth. What were you afraid would happen if you had spoken up?
- What would it mean to love someone fully and still refuse to disappear for them?

Affirmation

You did not fail at love. You loved with everything you had. The problem was never the size of your love it was that you forgot to include yourself in it. You are allowed to be loved back. You are allowed to require it.

Remember Her

The woman who ignored her instincts to keep the peace was not weak. She was doing the best she could with what she knew. Now you know more.

CHAPTER THREE

The Weight Women Carry

She weighed one pound and one ounce when they pulled her into the world.

That was only because of the fluids. When they weighed her again in the NICU, after the fluids had settled, the number changed. Eleven ounces. My daughter came into this world weighing eleven ounces. Less than a pound. Less than some people's breakfast.

I was on magnesium for the preeclampsia and the epidural was still in my system when they did the C-section, so the first moments of her life are something I received secondhand. My mother was in that room and she told me later what she saw. She said the baby came out pink. And then almost immediately she turned gray. Or blue. That particular shade that means the body is struggling to do the thing bodies are supposed to do automatically.

They showed her to me briefly a glimpse, a moment, the kind of thing you try to hold onto but can't quite grip because your mind is still foggy and your body has just been through something enormous. And then she was gone. Into the incubator. Into the NICU. Into a world of machines and nurses and interventions that I was not yet cleared to follow her into.

I went to sleep.

Not because I wasn't terrified. But because my body had nothing left.

It was two days before I could walk to her.

The first day they would not let me out of the bed. My blood pressure needed to stabilize. My body needed to begin the long process of recovering from a pregnancy that had nearly killed us both. I lay in that hospital bed knowing she was somewhere in that building, fighting, and I could not get to her.

The second day I got up.

I held the walls.

I am not being poetic when I say that. I literally pressed my hands against the hospital walls and used them to hold myself upright as I walked down the hallway to the NICU. My legs were not fully cooperating. My body was not ready. But I was going to my daughter and nothing was going to stop me from getting there.

The first time I saw her through the incubator I was not prepared for what I found.

She was under a blue light the kind they use for jaundice with tiny coverings over her eyes because her eyes were not yet developed enough to handle the light. Her lungs were not developed. Her ears were not developed. Her entire body was a work in progress, a life that had arrived before the world was ready for her, or maybe before she was ready for the world.

I looked at her hand. Her entire hand fingers and all was the size of my nail bed. And I have small hands.

I stood there looking at this tiny perfect impossible person and the only thought in my mind was: I am only going to have this moment. Not that she was going to make it. Not that we were going to get through this.

Just the terror of believing that this glimpse through the glass might be all I got. That we had come this far all of it, the bed rest, the preeclampsia, the emergency surgery, all of it and I was standing here watching her go in and out of consciousness under a blue light and she was not going to make it.

I was not ready to lose her.

I was also not ready to say that out loud to anyone.

So I didn't.

What I carried during those ten months is something I have never fully put into words. Not because I can't find them but because for a long time I didn't think I was allowed to say them. I was the strong one. I was the mother. I was the one who was supposed to be holding it together, and admitting what was actually happening inside me felt like a betrayal of that role.

So let me say it now.

I was terrified every single day. Not the visible kind of terror that people can see and respond to. The deep quiet kind that lives underneath your functioning, underneath your smile, underneath the steady voice you use when you talk to the doctors. I was afraid every day that I was going to walk into that room and something would have changed overnight. That the call I was not ready for was coming.

I was angry in ways I did not have permission to express. Angry at the situation. Angry at the helplessness. Angry that the person who was supposed to be standing beside me in the fullest sense of that word was physically present but somewhere else entirely. He was there. He came. He sat in the room. But there is a difference between a body in a chair and a partner in a crisis, and I felt that difference every single day without saying it to anyone.

I was lonely in a room full of people.

That is the particular loneliness of being the strong one. Everyone around you believes you are fine because you have trained them to believe it. You have never shown them the underneath. You have been so consistent in your strength that the people who love you have stopped checking because they trust that you would tell them if something was wrong.

I would not have told them.

I told myself it was not the time. My daughter needed me focused. The relationship needed me steady. Life outside the hospital still required attention bills, logistics, the basic machinery of existing in the world while your entire heart lived inside a NICU incubator. There was no space in any of that for my fear to exist out loud.

So I carried it. All of it. Every day.

We started at a Hospital in Arlington. That first hospital was what they called a barnyard style NICU all the incubators in one shared room, no private space, and I had to leave every single night. I could not stay. There was no bed for me. I would go home in the evenings knowing she was there alone and that was its own particular kind of weight.

Then they called me one night and told me I needed to come back.

They had called before multiple times and each call was its own small heart attack, its own sprint to the car, its own desperate drive back to a room I could not bear to be away from. But this call was different. This time when I got there they told me she was not going to make it through the night.

They said they needed to find a hospital that could care for her properly, a facility better equipped for a baby this small, this fragile, this early.
And then they said they did not think she would survive the ambulance ride to get there.
I want to tell you what happened inside me when they said that.
I shut it down.
Not the fear the fear was there, enormous and roaring underneath everything. But I shut down the part of me that was listening to the limitation. I was not going to sit in a room and receive a verdict about my daughter's life from people who were telling me what was not possible. I said: find the hospital. Put her in the ambulance. She will make it. That is not a question. That is what is happening.
They looked at me the way people look at a woman they think is in denial.
I was not in denial. I was in faith. There is a difference.
She made the ambulance ride. Of course she did.

The Cook children's hospital in Fort Worth changed everything.

Every baby had their own room. Every mother had space to stay. And for the next nine months, that room became my home. I did not leave more than a handful of times. The counselors and social workers would come in and gently suggest that I had a husband at home, a relationship that needed tending, a life outside those walls.

I heard them. And I had nothing to say to that.

My daughter was fighting for her life. There was nothing outside of those walls that required my attention more than she did. Nothing.

I slept beside her incubator. I talked to her through the clear walls long conversations about nothing and everything, about the life we were going to have when we got out of there, about the woman she was going to become. I sang to her. Softly, consistently, so that my voice became the most familiar sound in her world. I wanted her to know I was there. I wanted whatever part of her that could receive it to know that she was not alone.

She was not going to be alone.

They called her the little diva on the floor.

The nurses said it with a kind of exhausted affection the way you talk about someone who constantly keeps you on your toes and you love them anyway. She had a gift for setting off every alarm in the room and then being completely fine by the time everyone came running. She kept them all alert. She kept them all on their toes.

But the day that tested everything was the day of the surgery.

She had progressed enough that she needed a trach and a G-tube procedures to help her breathe and eat in ways her body was still learning to do on its own. They decided to do both surgeries at the same time. We walked with the doctors as they took her down. We waited. They came back and said the surgery had gone well.

She came back swollen they said that was normal and a nurse was working to fit her for the small clasp that holds the trach in place.

I was standing there waiting. Waiting to sit beside her. Waiting for this part to be over so I could just be with my daughter.

I do not know exactly what happened. Whether the nurse moved too quickly or her head was not properly supported or the Velcro from the clasp scratched the back of her neck and made her flinch. What I know is that one moment she was there and the next moment every alarm in the room went off in a different way than they had ever gone off before.

She flatlined.

The sound of that word does not capture what it does to a mother's body. It is not just fear. It is something that happens below fear, in a place you did not know existed until that moment. I had held myself together through about 6 months of terror. Through the phone calls in the night. Through the ambulance ride they said she would not survive. Through every setback and every scare and every morning I woke up not knowing what the day would bring. And in that moment I came completely undone.

I screamed. I cried. I could not be in that room. I ran actually ran down the hallway trying to get to the doors, to get out, to get somewhere that was not inside that moment. I hit the doors and they would not open fast enough and I dropped to the floor right there in that carpeted back hallway and I just fell apart. Completely. Loudly. Without any of the quiet composure I had maintained for months.

A nurse followed me. A counselor came. Someone said to call her father he had left after the surgery because it was done, because he had somewhere to be.

He had somewhere to be.

I was on the floor of a hospital hallway and he had somewhere to be.

I am not saying this to condemn him. I am saying it because it is the truest picture I have of what those months actually looked like from the inside. The physical presence that was not quite partnership. The body that was there and the heart that was somewhere else. And me, alone on that floor, screaming for my daughter to come back.

She came back.

Of course she did. My daughter did not come into this world to leave it quietly. She came back and the nurses shook their heads and called her the diva and said this is exactly why we love her and exactly why she exhausts us.

She still has the scar. Right at the back of her head, just under the hairline where the Velcro caught her. Her hair does not grow there. Just a small patch of smooth skin that tells the story of the day she scared me more than I have ever been scared in my life and then came back like it was nothing.

She came back.

And so, eventually, did I.

What nobody tells you about being the strong one is that strength without support is just another word for alone.

I had my mother. I had my family. They showed up in the ways that families show up present, loving, doing what they could. And that mattered. That held me in ways I am still grateful for. But there is a specific kind of support that only comes from the person who is supposed to be your partner. The person who chose this life with you.

The person who is supposed to look at you across a hospital room and say without words: I see what this is costing you and I am not going anywhere.

I did not have that.

And I told myself I was fine without it.

I was not fine. I was surviving. I was functioning. I was doing what mothers do when there is no other option showing up, day after day, with whatever was left in me, pouring it into that incubator through the walls, singing songs and saying prayers and refusing to receive any version of the story where she did not make it.

But fine is not the same as whole. And somewhere in those ten months of being everyone's anchor, of being the one who held it all together while nobody held me, I drifted further from myself than I even realized.

I thought I was being strong.

I was actually disappearing.

And the terrifying thing about disappearing slowly is that you do not notice it until one day you look up and the woman you used to be is so far behind you that you can barely make out her face.

She was still there. Waiting. She never left.

But I had stopped looking for her.

And that is the weight that no one talks about. Not the weight of the hard seasons. Not the weight of the medical bills or the sleepless nights or the fear that never fully goes away. The weight of losing yourself so gradually, so quietly, so respectably in the name of strength, in the name of love, in the name of being the woman everyone needed you to be that by the time you notice it you have been gone for years.

That is the weight women carry.
And it is time to put it down.

Remember Her Reflection

- When have you been the strong one for so long that you forgot you were also allowed to need something?
- What have you been carrying in silence that deserves to finally be said out loud?
- Who has been your anchor in your hardest seasons — and have you ever let them know what that meant to you?
- What would it feel like to let someone hold you for a change — not because you are weak, but because you are human?

Affirmation

You were not built to carry the world alone. The fact that you have does not mean you were supposed to. Needing support is not weakness. It is the most honest thing a human being can do. You are allowed to be held. You have always been allowed to be held.

Remember Her

Strength was never meant to mean solitude. The most powerful thing you can do is let someone in — starting with yourself.

CHAPTER FOUR

The Breaking Point

I want to tell you something about hope.

Hope is not always a bright thing. Sometimes it is the quiet stubborn thing that keeps you in a situation long after the evidence has told you to go. Sometimes hope is the story you tell yourself in the dark the one that starts with maybe and ends with eventually and you hold onto it not because it is likely but because the alternative is admitting something you are not yet ready to face.

For years, hope was the most expensive thing I owned.

The phone call happened on a day like any other day in the NICU.

My daughter was in her incubator. The machines were doing what machines do. I was sitting in that room the way I sat in that room every day present, watchful, tired in the particular way that becomes your baseline when you have been living inside a hospital for months.

He had been there. He left. Said he was going home to rest. Said he was exhausted. I understood. I told him that was fine.

The phone did not hang up.

I did not realize it at first. The line was still open and I was not paying attention to it, just sitting there in the quiet hum of that room. And then I heard something. A voice. A woman's voice. A voice I did not recognize and had never heard before in my life.

He was not at home.

He was at lunch. With her.

I sat there for a moment making sure I was hearing what I was hearing. Making sure I was not misunderstanding. I was not misunderstanding.

I hung up. And then I called him back.

I said: do you know you didn't hang up? Do you know that I heard exactly where you are? I know you lied to me.

And he did what people do when they are caught and not ready to be accountable. He talked his way around it. Just a friend. Needed a break. Just lunch. Someone I don't know, never heard of, just a person he happened to go have lunch with. Nothing to worry about.

This was not the first time.

There had been another day another visit, another goodbye, another I made it home safely that turned out to be something else entirely. A friend's house. Watching a game. Which sounds innocent enough until you understand that the pattern was the lying. Not just the where but the automatic, reflexive, practiced lying. The ease of it.

I cried that day. Quietly, the way I had learned to cry in that hospital contained, careful, conscious of the tiny person in the incubator who I believed could feel everything I felt even through the glass. I went to my daughter. My little best friend who was fighting for her life.

I sat with her and I let myself fall apart just enough to keep going.
And then within a few weeks I did what I had trained myself to do.
I pushed it down. I forgave him. I chose the baby. I chose the future I was still hoping we could build.
Hope is expensive. I kept paying anyway.

We got married about a year after she came home.
It was not the wedding I had imagined as a girl. There was no ceremony with flowers and a reception and a dress I had dreamed about. We went to the courthouse. A close friend was our witness the woman who would later become my daughter's godmother. That was it. Small and quiet and official.
And standing there I felt both things at once.
I felt hope. Genuine hope. The kind that is not naive but determined the belief that the act of choosing each other formally, legally, permanently might be the thing that finally made us solid. I had seen what we had survived together. The NICU. The fear. The nights when we did not know if she was going to make it. I thought that kind of survival had to mean something. I thought we had earned something real on the other side of all that pain.
And underneath the hope, quiet and persistent, was the doubt.
The knowledge I had been carrying for months sitting right there underneath everything. The phone call. The lies. The pattern I had seen clearly and then talked myself out of seeing. It was there on my wedding day the way it had been there every day present, patient, waiting for me to finally stop negotiating with it.

I chose hope. I said the words. I signed the name.
And for a little while, it was better. The way things sometimes get better when you make a decision not because the problems are gone but because the decision itself creates a kind of momentum, a forward motion that feels like progress. We were married. We were building. We were going to make this work.

The pudding company was born in a friend's kitchen.
After our daughter came home from the NICU in October of 2014 one week before my birthday, which I took as a gift from the universe I had a few remaining sculpted cake orders to fulfill and then I was done with that chapter of my business. I could not give the cakes what they required and give my daughter what she required at the same time, and she won that decision without a contest.
But I was still a woman with a creative mind and a business spirit and I was not going to sit still.
She was known for her banana pudding. People had been saying it for years that my pudding was something different, something that deserved its own spotlight. And sitting in that friend's kitchen after being displaced and between homes, while he went to work, while our daughter was playing, I started writing things down. Scripting it out the way I would later learn to script my life. I ordered jars. I tested recipes. Red velvet pudding. Blueberry. Strawberry banana. Every flavor a possibility, a new expression of something that had always been mine.
I took pictures. I built the vision out on paper before it existed in the world.

When I showed him he got excited too. He came up with the name because I could not find one that felt right. I had the recipe and the vision and the fire. He had the name and the willingness to go stand at a farmers market and sell. We divided the labor the way partners are supposed to. I created. He sold. Together we built something that started to get real traction.

We got into Central Market. We were creating a buzz. We even got an audition for Shark Tank — which still amazes me when I say it out loud because this was a business born on a friend's kitchen counter, built on a recipe people had loved for years, driven by a woman who needed something of her own.

The thought behind all of it was our daughter.

They had told us she might never reach certain milestones. That her path might look different from other children's paths. That the things most people take for granted might require different roads for her. And we looked at each other and decided that if the world was not going to make space for her automatically, we would build her something she could always come home to. A legacy. A company with her name written into its foundation even before she was old enough to understand what that meant.

That was the dream. And for a time, the dream was working. Then the partners came. And then the debt. And then the slow unraveling of something we had built with our hands.

I will not go into every detail of what happened to the business because this is not a story about a business failing. It is a story about what happens to a woman when everything falls apart at the same time and she is the only one still trying to hold any of it together.

He went abroad to pursue something else. A new opportunity, a different way to generate income. I supported that. I stayed. I kept the household running. I managed our daughter's care, her appointments, her therapies, my stepsons care. I did all of it. I kept saying yes to carrying more because that was what I knew how to do.

When he came back and the new venture had not produced what we needed I was the one who said: I think you should get a job. We have a home. We have children depending on us. We need consistent income and we need it now.

He looked at me and said: no. You get a job. I'll stay home to continue this pursuit.

I want you to sit with that for a moment.

I want you to feel what those words feel like landing in a body that has spent years carrying everything. Years of being the emotional anchor, the creative engine, the household manager, the primary caregiver for a medically complex child. Years of quiet and forgiveness and pushing things down and choosing hope over truth.

You get a job. I'll stay home.

In that moment something in me did not break. It clarified.

This man did not love me the way I needed to be loved. I had known that for a long time. But in that moment I understood something deeper he was not going to protect me. He was not going to provide for me. He was not going to show up for this family the way this family needed him to show up. And I had been waiting, patiently, faithfully, quietly, for him to become someone he was never going to become.

The next eviction came not long after.

I will not dress that up or soften it. We lost our home. They put our belongings on the street and we loaded what mattered into the back of the car and left the rest. I lost things that day that I will never get back. Not just objects though those were real losses too but the last remaining piece of the story I had been telling myself. The one where we were going to be okay. Where it was all going to work out. Where the hope I had invested for years was going to pay off.

That story ended on a sidewalk with our belongings on it.

We stay with av friend for a week then We went to stay with his brother and his wife. And I remember the first day there, standing by the door, trying to give him a kiss as he was leaving. He pulled back. Just slightly. Just enough. Then he caught himself and gave me something that was not quite a kiss.

His sister in law saw it. She looked at him and then at me and then back at him and she did not say a word. She did not have to.

Something in me went completely still.

Not sad. Not angry. Just still. The way a decision feels when it stops being a question.

I was done.

I did not tell him.

I started doing notary work quietly, putting money aside that he did not know about. Not much we did not have much but enough. I researched how to file for divorce without lawyers. Found a company that handled uncontested divorces, figured out the cost, figured out what I needed to do. I presented him with the paperwork when I was ready.

I said: I already paid my half. I need you to pay yours so we can finalize this.

There were arguments. There were difficult conversations. There were moments where old habits rose up in me the urge to soften, to make it easier for him, to be the good woman one more time. But I had a number in my head and a plan in my hands and an apartment I had found and a deposit I had scraped together and a date I was moving toward.

I was not just leaving a marriage. I was executing a plan I had built in secret with the quiet determination of a woman who has finally decided that her life belongs to her.

The divorce was finalized. One week later I was moving into my own apartment with my daughter.

The thing I was most afraid of was not starting over.

It was not being alone or rebuilding from nothing or facing the practical mountain of a woman with damaged credit and an eviction on her record trying to find housing and create stability from scratch.

What I was most afraid of was my daughter.

I had grown up in a home where my father's presence was complicated there but not always there in the ways that mattered. I had told myself I would not repeat that. I had chosen this man to build a family with partly because I wanted her to have what I was not always sure I had. And leaving meant admitting that the thing I had tried to build had not become what I needed it to be. It meant she was going to grow up in two homes. It meant the cycle I had tried so hard to break was breaking in a different way than I planned.

And underneath that fear was a deeper one.
I was terrified she would grow up and love the way I had loved. That she would learn from watching me that a woman absorbs things in silence. That she would internalize the lesson I had been living that love means disappearing, that staying is strength, that a good woman keeps the peace at the cost of her own.
That fear was the final push.
I did not leave for myself alone. I left so she would have something different to learn. So when she was old enough to watch how her mother moved through the world she would see a woman who chose herself. A woman who decided her peace was worth protecting. A woman who built something from nothing not because she had to but because she knew she could.
I left so she would know that was possible.
And on the day I carried our things into that apartment just the two of us, just what we needed, just the beginning I made her a promise she was too young to understand.
You will never watch me shrink for anyone.
Not ever again.

Remember Her Reflection

- Have you ever held onto hope long after the evidence asked you to let go? What were you most afraid of admitting?
- What is the thing you have been preparing for in secret the plan you have not told anyone about yet?
- What would it mean to leave not in anger but in love, love for yourself and love for the future you deserve?
- What do you want the children or young women watching you to learn from how you handle this season?

Affirmation

Leaving is not failure. Sometimes leaving is the most loving and courageous act available to you. You do not need anyone's permission to choose a life that is worthy of you. The plan you have been building quietly in your heart is valid. The door you are walking toward is real.

Remember Her

You did not leave because you stopped loving. You left because you finally loved yourself enough to stop accepting less than you deserved. That is not weakness. That is the bravest thing a woman can do.

CHAPTER FIVE

The Wandering Years

The first night in my new apartment we slept on an air mattress.

Not because I had not planned. I had planned everything the deposit saved in secret, the first month's rent set aside, the application submitted to a complex in Rowlett that would accept me despite the eviction on my record and the credit score that told a story I was still in the middle of rewriting. I had planned. But planning and arriving are two different things, and when we walked through that door with our suitcases and the few things we had carried out of his brother's house, the apartment was empty in a way that was both frightening and sacred.

Just us. Just our things. Just the beginning.

I had made sure her room came together first. That was non-negotiable. Whatever else I had to figure out, whatever I had to go without, my daughter was going to have a space that felt like hers. Pink bedding. Nightstands. Curtains. The kind of room that tells a child she is thought of, she is provided for, she is loved. I built her sanctuary before I built anything else.

My room was a bed frame and a mattress and walls I had not yet figured out what to do with.

The rest of the apartment was sparse in the way that starting over is always sparse. A small couch. In the space where a dining room table might have been, I set up my work area my laptop, my notary equipment, the tools of the income I had been building quietly before I ever told anyone I was leaving. That little makeshift office in the dining room was not glamorous. But it was mine. Every piece of it was mine.

The apartment was cold the way empty spaces are cold. Not temperature the Texas heat took care of that. But the particular chill of a place that does not yet have enough life in it. Not enough furniture to fill the corners. Not enough history on the walls. Not enough of the accumulated warmth that a home builds over time.

I did not care.

Because when I walked out onto the balcony and looked out at the lake, something in my chest that had been clenched for years began slowly, cautiously to open.

There was a lake. Right there. I could see it from my balcony. On the mornings when the light hit the water a certain way I would stand out there and take pictures because I could not believe this view belonged to my life now. That this quiet, this sky, this water that I had access to this simply by stepping outside my own door.

I stood on that balcony and breathed in a way I had not breathed in a very long time.

This was mine. We were going to be okay.

Let me be honest about what okay actually looked like.

We were on government assistance. I was doing remote online notary work. The rent was getting paid. There was food.

By the metrics that matter most we were surviving but surviving and thriving are not the same thing and I was not going to pretend otherwise to myself even when I was pretending otherwise to the world.

The weeks my daughter was with her father were the hardest and the strangest. The apartment was so quiet in those weeks that I did not always know what to do with myself. Some days I would sit in that quiet and actually rest really rest, the kind your body needs after years of running on adrenaline and determination. Some days I would go to my mother's house just to be around people, to let my daughter's aunties and grandparents fold us both into the noise and warmth of family. Some days I reached out to people I probably should not have reached out to conversations I was having not because those people were right for me but because I was searching for something to fill a space I did not yet understand.

I was looking for a sense of belonging.

I did not realize yet that what I was looking for was inside me. That the belonging I was chasing in other people's attention was something I was going to have to build inside myself first. That realization was still coming. In those early wandering months I just knew I was untethered in a way that felt both free and terrifying, and some nights I handled that freedom well and some nights I did not.

That is the honest truth of the wandering years. It is not a straight line toward the light. It is a crooked, doubling-back, sometimes-sliding-backward journey that eventually eventually starts to move in one direction.

My daughter was six years old when we moved into that apartment.

Six years old and already one of the most remarkable human beings I have ever known. She had graduated from her trach. She had graduated from her feeding tube. The tiny eleven-ounce fighter who had kept the entire NICU floor on their toes had grown into a little girl who woke up every single morning happy. Dancing. Singing. Moving through the world with a joy that I could not always explain given everything she had been through but that I accepted as the gift it was.

She still had milestones she was working toward. We did ABA therapy together. We had shared counseling. We navigated the ongoing work of helping her body and mind catch up to the life she was living so fully and so joyfully. That work was real and it required presence and consistency and advocacy that never stopped.

But she was here. She was thriving in her own particular way. And watching her do that watching this child who was not supposed to survive the ambulance ride dance around our sparse little apartment in her pink room gave me something to hold onto on the days when I did not have much else.

Co-parenting, in those early days, was actually manageable. We worked better apart than we had together. I already knew he had moved on and that clarity made the logistics easier there was no false hope on the table, no confusion about what we were to each other. We were her parents. That was the whole job. And when I could keep that as the focus, we could do it.

The harder thing to navigate was what nobody prepares you for when you become a single mother in the full sense of the word.

There is no one to tap out to.

Before, even in the most difficult seasons, there had been another body in the house. Another person I could theoretically, at least turn to and say: I need a moment. I need five minutes. I need someone else to handle this right now. That option disappears when it is just you. On the days I did not want to get up and there were days I did not want to get up I got up anyway. Not because I had conquered those feelings but because a six year old does not know you are struggling and she should not have to know. She deserved a mother who showed up. So I showed up. Every day. Even on the days it cost me everything I had.

That daily showing up invisible, unwitnessed, unremarked upon was some of the hardest work I have ever done.

The moment I first felt like myself again did not happen in the apartment.

It happened before I even got there.

I was packing the car. Loading what we were taking the suitcases, the boxes, the things I had decided we were bringing into this new chapter. I had already paid the deposit. I had already secured the apartment. I had already done the quiet invisible work of preparing for this moment over months of careful saving and planning. And standing there next to that packed car, knowing that on the other side of this drive was a space that belonged to us just us something shifted.

I thought: it is onward and upward from here.

Not that everything was figured out. Not that the fear was gone or the uncertainty had resolved itself or the journey ahead was going to be easy. None of that was true. But for the first time in a very long time I felt the specific aliveness that comes from knowing you are moving toward something you chose. Not running from. Moving toward.

I was not all the way back to myself. I want to be honest about that. The woman I was becoming was still far down the road, still being assembled from pieces I had not yet found. But that moment by the car that was the first signal. The first small clear note of a song I had not heard in years.

She is still in there. She is still there.

Let's go.

What I did not expect to grieve was myself.

Not the marriage I had made peace with the end of that before I ever signed the papers. Not the business, not the life we had tried to build, not even the dream of the long lasting partnership I had spent years hoping we would find our way to.

What caught me completely off guard was having to grieve the story I had been telling myself.

The one that said if I was good enough, patient enough, loving enough, it would eventually become what I needed it to be. The one that said the problem was fixable and I was the one who could fix it. The one where my worth was tied to whether I could make something work that was not working and the terrifying inverse of that, which was this:

If it did not work, maybe the problem was me.

That was the grief I did not see coming. That quiet, corrosive belief that I had not been worthy enough. That something about me my neediness, my expectations, my inability to be content with what was being offered had contributed to the failure. I had to grieve the version of that story where I was the problem. And I had to grieve it slowly, honestly, with mirror work and scripting and long private conversations with myself that were more difficult than any argument I had ever had with anyone else.

Looking at yourself in a mirror and saying: you are enough. You were always enough. What happened to you was not a verdict on your worth.

Saying it before you believe it. Saying it especially before you believe it.

That is the work of the wandering years that nobody puts on the timeline. The inner archaeology. The excavation of all the stories you absorbed and internalized and built your self-concept on top of stories that were never true, told to you by circumstances and by people who were also just trying to survive their own wandering.

I was not unworthy.

I had just forgotten, somewhere in all those years of shrinking and staying quiet and choosing everyone else first, that my worth was never up for negotiation in the first place.

It was never something I had to earn.
It was something I had always had.
The wandering years were the years I had to go back and find that truth buried under the Good Woman rules, under the hospital months, under the years of carrying everything alone, under the eviction and the packed car and the sparse apartment and the air mattress on the first night.
It was under all of it.
Waiting.
The way she is always waiting.
The way she always waits for us to come back to her.

Remember Her Reflection

- What season of your life has felt most like wandering uncertain, in between, not quite who you were and not yet who you are becoming?
- What story about your own worth have you been grieving without naming it as grief?
- What does your version of the lake view look like the small beautiful thing that reminds you that peace is possible?
- What would it mean to stop looking for belonging in other people and start building it inside yourself?

Affirmation

You are allowed to be in the middle. You are allowed to not have it figured out. The wandering is not evidence that you are lost it is evidence that you are honest enough to admit you are still finding your way. That honesty is its own kind of courage. Keep going. She is at the end of this road waiting for you.

Remember Her

The wandering years are not wasted years. They are the years you finally stopped performing and started becoming. Every uncertain step was a step toward yourself.

CHAPTER SIX

The First Night of the Rest of Me

It took five years.

From the day I signed the divorce papers and moved into that sparse apartment in Rowlett with two suitcases and an air mattress, to the day I loaded a moving truck and drove sixteen hours toward a life I had built on purpose it took five years. And I want to tell you about every season of that journey because the path from broken to becoming is never as clean or as straight as people make it sound when they tell their stories from the other side.

The Rowlett apartment was the beginning. Beautiful in its own way — that lake view, that balcony, that first deep breath of peace. But I had bitten off more than I could chew financially and I knew it. The two bedroom that I had gotten so my daughter could have her own sanctuary was stretching me in ways I could not sustain. So I made the first of many financially honest decisions and transitioned into a one bedroom.

My daughter and I shared a bed.

I want you to understand that I am not telling you that as a hardship story. I am telling you because it is the truth of what rebuilding actually looks like. It is not always the cinematic moment of the woman standing in her own space victorious.

Sometimes it is a mother and her daughter in a one bedroom apartment sharing a bed and making it work because making it work is what you do.

I kept the roof over our heads. I kept us fed. I kept moving. But I also got honest with myself about what I needed. Not just financially structurally. I needed support. I needed a foundation under me while I built what I was trying to build. And so when my lease was up I made a decision that my pride initially resisted but my wisdom eventually accepted.

I moved back home with my parents.

I did not do all of this to live a life of struggle. That was never the goal. The goal was to find my power and in order to do that I needed to stop pretending I could do everything alone and start utilizing the support that was available to me. My parents' house gave me and my daughter community. It gave her grandparents and aunties around her. It gave me breathing room. And in that breathing room I did something I had been wanting to do since I closed the doors on the business that had been taken from under me.

I rebuilt the pudding company.

This time it was entirely mine. In the divorce decree everything had been turned over to me. My recipe. My brand. My vision. The thing I had created in a friend's kitchen while testing flavors and ordering jars while he was at work that was mine from the beginning and now it was officially, legally, completely mine.

I went through the process properly this time. Got my LLC. Got my licenses. Secured a commercial kitchen.

Did everything by the book because this was not a side project. This was my legacy. This was what I was passing down.

And then I went back to the farmers market.

My sister came with me that first day. I remember standing there at the booth with my product and my jars and everything I had built back up from scratch, and the people came. Not strangers people who recognized me. People who stopped and looked at the booth and then looked at me and their faces did something I was not prepared for.

They were happy to see me.

Not just pleasant. Not just polite. Genuinely, warmly, personally happy.

One after another they said some version of the same thing: we have been waiting for you to come back. Two years. Three years. We kept looking for you. Your pudding there is nothing like it.

I stood there behind that booth and felt something shift in me that I do not have a perfect word for. It was not just gratitude. It was recognition. The kind that comes from the outside and lands somewhere deep inside and confirms something you had almost stopped believing.

It was always you, Kendra.

Not the partnership. Not the business structure. Not the name someone else came up with or the farmer's market booth someone else stood in front of. The product, the recipe, the thing people had driven back to find after three years of absence that was you. That was always you.

I had spent so much time believing I could not do the sales part.

That I needed to stay behind the scenes. That the front-facing part of the business was someone else's role and I was better off in the kitchen where it was safe and familiar. But standing there that day, watching people light up when they saw me, I understood something I had been resisting for years.

I am my brand.

The pudding is an expression of me. The warmth people feel when they taste it is the warmth I put into it. You cannot separate the product from the person and I had been trying to for years hiding behind the kitchen, letting someone else be the face, making myself smaller than the thing I had created.

Not anymore.

That farmers market was my butterfly moment. The first time I stood fully in front of something I had built and said this is mine and I am not stepping back from it.

I got a job in 2023. A position I had worked toward, studied for, earned certifications for during those months at my parents' house when I was quietly building while everyone around me thought I was just getting back on my feet. The position paid more than enough. More than enough to take care of her. More than enough to give her not just what she needed but what she wanted. More than enough to move out and build a comfortable life and finally finally feel the financial ground solid under my feet.

And immediately I knew I wanted to leave Texas.

I had wanted to leave from the moment things fell apart. The urge to run had been there for years. But I had learned the difference between running and declaring between leaving in desperation and leaving in readiness and I was not going to repeat the pattern of moving toward something before I was built enough to sustain it.

So I waited. I built. I prepared.

And then I had the conversation.

Co-parenting across state lines is not simple. I could not just take my daughter and go there were legal agreements, parental rights, a relationship with her father that I had worked hard to keep functional for her sake. I started the conversation with him and he pushed back. Negotiations took longer than I wanted. I had hoped to leave in 2023 and it stretched into 2024. But eventually with patience and legal documentation and a restructured co-parenting agreement that we got notarized we reached an arrangement that worked. She would still have fifty-fifty time with both of us. She would still have her father. She would still have both of her parents present in her life even from different states.

By 2024 I was ready.

I was supposed to have company on the drive.

My mother had planned to come with me sixteen hours of highway is a long way for a woman and her daughter to travel alone and my family wanted someone there with me. But life does not always cooperate with plans. Someone got sick. My mother could not make it. And I stood there on the morning of my departure with a packed moving truck and a daughter and a choice.

I chose to go anyway.

Everyone had something to say about it. Are you sure you want to do this alone? All sixteen hours? Just the two of you? And I heard every concern and I held every one of them with love and I got in that car anyway because my new life was not in Texas. The start of who I was becoming was not in Texas. And I was leaving by any means necessary.

We left at six in the morning.

The first hours were full of the particular energy of beginnings the excitement of motion, the music, my daughter settled in beside me with her iPad, the road opening up ahead of us like a sentence that had not yet been finished. I felt ready. I felt like myself. I felt like a woman who had spent five years building toward exactly this moment and was finally living it.

And then the tooth started.

I do not know how else to say this except the way I felt it that toothache was not random. It started on that drive with an intensity that made me question everything. Why now. Why this day. Why would my body choose this particular moment to remind me of pain.

I believe in signs. I believe the body speaks what the spirit is processing. And what I believe that toothache was saying to me in the language of physical pain, in the only language loud enough to make me pay attention was this: push through. The ceiling is right here. Push through it.

There were miles of that drive where the tears just fell. Not sobbing. Just tears rolling down my face while I kept my hands on the wheel and kept moving. We are going to make it. We are going to make it. I said it out loud sometimes and sometimes just in my head but I said it consistently the way you say the thing you need to believe until you believe it.

My daughter was a trooper. She did not know the full weight of what her mother was carrying on that drive. She knew we were going somewhere new and exciting and she had her iPad and her snacks and her faith in me that was so uncomplicated and so complete that it made me want to be worthy of it.

We made our stops. We kept going. We pushed through the wall.

We arrived at one in the morning.

The leasing office was not going to open until nine. So we checked into a hotel exhausted in the particular way that is beyond tiredness, the kind that lives in your bones. I got my daughter settled into bed. And then before I let myself sleep I did jumping jacks in that hotel room.

Fifteen minutes of jumping jacks and running in place at one in the morning in a hotel room in a new state.

Because I had driven sixteen hours with a toothache and tears on my face and I was not going to come all this way and not wake up. My blood pressure. My history. My body that had already been through so much. I was going to do everything in my power to make sure I woke up for the morning that was coming.

I set my alarm. I fell into the bed. I was out before I finished the thought.

Nine o'clock came and I was there.

I got the keys. My sister who had come down to help me was there. The movers came. Everything went in.

And by the time the last box was inside and the movers were gone and it was just us just me and my daughter and our things in this brand new space in this brand new city I took a breath.

Not a regular breath.

The kind that starts somewhere deeper than your lungs. The kind that your body takes when it finally finally believes it is safe.

I have arrived.

Not I have survived. Not I have made it through. I have arrived. As in: this is the destination. This is the place. This is the life I was building toward through every hard season, every quiet sacrifice, every moment I chose to keep going when stopping would have been so much easier.

I was beyond exhausted. Four hours of sleep the night before, sixteen hours of driving, moving everything in my body had nothing left. My one goal for that first night was to eat something and get into a bed and sleep. That was it. No profound moment of standing at a window looking at a new skyline. No journaling by candlelight. Just food and sleep and the deep animal comfort of being somewhere that belongs to you.

But even in that exhaustion maybe especially in that exhaustion I felt it.

The glow.

Not the external kind. Not the kind you put on for other people or perform for photographs. The internal kind. The kind that comes from the inside out when your life finally matches the vision you have been holding in your heart through years of uncertainty and loss and rebuilding.

I had done it.

I had done it.

Not because circumstances lined up perfectly. Not because someone rescued me or the path was clear or the journey was clean. But because I refused. I refused to stay where I was not growing. I refused to keep running before I was ready. I refused to let fear make the decision that courage was supposed to make. I refused to get on that highway with a toothache and tears and turn around.

I kept going.

And on the other side of the wall on the other side of the ceiling I had pushed through with nothing but determination and jumping jacks and a six year old girl asleep in the passenger seat was this.

My life.

The one I had chosen.

The one I had built.

The one that was finally, completely, unapologetically mine.

Taking the First Step

The first thing I want you to know is that reclaiming your life does not require a grand gesture. It does not require a perfect plan or a dramatic exit. It starts with something much quieter than that.

It starts with one decision you make for yourself today.

Maybe that decision is setting a boundary you have been avoiding. Maybe it is saying no to something that drains you without giving anything back. Maybe it is simply deciding that your peace matters enough to protect. Start there.

If you are in a season where you need to rebuild financially, start small and start now. Even saving twenty dollars a week is not about the amount it is about the message you are sending yourself. That you are worth planning for. That your future deserves investment. That you are not just surviving this season you are preparing for the next one.

And speak your truth first to yourself, then to the world. Write down the things you have been afraid to say out loud. Then read them back to yourself. There is something that shifts when you hear your own voice telling the truth. It reminds you that the truth was always there. You just needed permission to say it.

You are the one who gives that permission now.

Remember Her Reflection

- Is there a place, a decision, or a life that you have been preparing for but have not yet given yourself permission to move toward?
- What is the wall you are being asked to push through right now and what is waiting for you on the other side of it?
- What would it mean to stop waiting for the perfect conditions and start moving toward your life anyway?
- What is the one decision you could make today that your future self would thank you for?

Affirmation

You survived the nights that felt impossible. You got up when you had every reason to stay down. You built something from nothing and that is not luck. That is who you are. That has always been who you are. The life waiting for you on the other side of the wall is real. Keep driving.

Remember Her

There is no timeline for healing. There is no deadline for remembering. Only the quiet steady truth that the woman you are looking for has been here all along and she has been driving toward you this whole time.

CHAPTER SEVEN

Claiming What Was Always Mine

The first thing I do when I wake up is say thank you.

Not dramatically. Not with a long prayer or a formal ritual. Just the simple act of opening my eyes and before I reach for my phone or think about my schedule or let the day rush in I say thank you. And then I make a decision. I decide that today is going to be a good day. I even have a plaque in my kitchen that says it: today is a good day to have a good day. It sounds simple. It is simple. But simple is not the same as small.

That morning practice gratitude first, declaration second became the foundation of everything else I built in this new season. Because what I learned about reclaiming yourself is that it does not begin with the big dramatic moves. It begins in the first five minutes of the day before anyone else has any claim on your attention. It begins with the choice you make before your feet even hit the floor.

I choose this day. I choose this life. I choose myself.

That is not something the woman I used to be knew how to do.

That woman woke up already calculating. Already managing. Already trying to figure out how to navigate the day in a way that would keep everyone around her comfortable and the peace intact. Some mornings she did not want to get out of bed at all.

The depression that settled into those difficult years was not the loud visible kind it was the quiet kind that lives underneath the functioning, underneath the showing up, underneath the keeping it together. The kind that makes ordinary mornings feel like mountains.

This is not that anymore.

The rhythm of my mornings now has an ease to it that I do not take for granted for even one day. Because I know what the other kind of mornings feel like. I know the difference between waking up with dread and waking up with possibility. And the difference between those two experiences is not luck or circumstance or the absence of hard things in your life.

It is the internal work.

It is the daily, unglamorous, deeply personal practice of choosing yourself before the world gets a chance to choose for you.

My practices are simple. They are consistent. And they changed my life.

Journaling and scripting became my morning anchors. Not journaling in the way people imagine not just processing feelings or cataloguing the day. Scripting. Writing the future as if it is already happening. Describing the life I was moving toward in the present tense, in specific detail, as if I was already living inside it. I wake up every morning with peace. I provide abundantly for my daughter. I am a woman who knows her worth and does not negotiate it.

I wrote those things before they were fully true. I wrote them especially before they were fully true.

Because what I learned about the mind is that it does not always know the difference between what is happening and what is being vividly, consistently, emotionally imagined. You write the life. You feel the life. And slowly not overnight, not in a straight line, but surely you start making decisions that match what you have been writing.

The scripting was accompanied by mirror work. Standing in front of my reflection and saying things out loud that I did not yet fully believe but needed to hear in my own voice. Because there is something that happens when you hear yourself say not read, not think, but actually say out loud to your own face I am enough. I am worthy. I am exactly where I am supposed to be.

At first it felt strange. Uncomfortable in the way that truth sometimes feels when you have been living with a lie for so long that the truth sounds foreign. But I kept going. I kept standing there. I kept saying the words until they stopped feeling like something I was trying to convince myself of and started feeling like something I was simply remembering.

Because that is what it was. Not convincing. Remembering.

The body required its own conversation.

I want to be honest about this because I think women deserve honesty about what rebuilding actually looks like physically. I gained weight during those years of surviving. Food has always been a love language for me not just cooking it for other people but receiving comfort from it myself. And between the stress and the grief and the hormonal changes of moving into my forties and what I believe was the beginning of perimenopause, my body changed in ways I had to consciously choose to make peace with.

I started working with a personal trainer. Three days a week. Not to chase a body I used to have. Not to punish myself into a smaller size. But to begin a new relationship with the body that had carried me through everything through the pregnancy, through the NICU months, through the years of survival, through the sixteen hour drive with tears on my face and a toothache that would not quit.

This body deserved to be honored. Not criticized. Not compared to a younger version of itself. Honored.

I would look in the mirror and say it out loud: I love the body that got me here. Not the body I wanted or the body I used to have. The body that got me here. The one that survived the things it survived, carried what it carried, kept going when stopping would have been so much easier.

I am forty years old now. I am not twenty year old Kendra and I am not supposed to be. I am the Kendra who earned every year. Who lived inside every season. Who came out the other side of things that should have broken her and somehow somehow did not break.

That woman deserves love. Starting with mine.

The most powerful thing I learned to say in this season was the smallest word in the English language.

No.

I say it freely now. Immediately. Without the lengthy internal negotiation that used to accompany every request that did not feel right. If I do not feel it in my spirit if something in my body responds to a yes with that particular tightening that tells me the yes is not true I have learned to go back and correct it.

Even if I already said yes.
Even if saying no feels inconvenient or disappointing or requires a conversation I would rather avoid. I have learned that a yes that is not true is more expensive than a no that is honest. I have learned that I do not have to explain myself. I can simply say: I apologize but I am not going to be able to do that. And let that be the whole sentence.
This sounds simple. For me it was revolutionary.
I was a yes woman for most of my life. Yes to keep the peace. Yes to avoid conflict. Yes from a hospital bed. Yes even when everything inside me was screaming something different. Learning to say no cleanly, kindly, without guilt and without a three paragraph explanation was one of the most profound acts of self reclamation I have ever performed.
Because every no that is true is a yes to yourself.
And I had been saying yes to everyone else for so long that I had forgotten I was allowed to be on the list.

Financial independence does not feel the way people describe it from the outside.
From the outside it looks like a number. An income bracket. A savings account balance. But from the inside from inside the body of a woman who once had her belongings put out on the street, who saved notary money in secret to pay for her own divorce, who moved into a one bedroom apartment and shared a bed with her daughter to keep the roof over their heads financial independence feels like one thing.
Freedom.

Not just the freedom to buy things. The freedom to stop being afraid. The freedom to wake up in the morning and not spend the first fifteen minutes calculating whether you are going to make it through the month. The freedom to look at your daughter and know not hope, not pray, not cross your fingers but know that she is provided for. That her needs are met. That her wants are possible. That the generational wealth you want to create for her is not a dream you are postponing it is a plan you are executing.

I asked myself a question during this season that changed how I thought about money entirely: what is the lifestyle I desire? Not the lifestyle I thought I could afford or the lifestyle I thought I deserved or the lifestyle that seemed realistic given where I had been. The lifestyle I desired. The one that would make me feel free and comfortable and like the woman I was becoming.

And then I figured out what number at minimum would get me to the baseline of that life.

That question gave me a target. And having a target changed everything because I stopped making financial decisions out of fear and started making them out of intention. There is a profound difference between the two. Fear-based financial decisions keep you small and reactive. Intention-based financial decisions make you the architect of your own life.

I am not where I ultimately want to be. I want to be honest about that. The generational wealth I am building takes time. The legacy I am creating for my daughter is still in progress. But I am so much closer than I was. And the distance between where I am and where I started the distance between the woman who could not pay for her own divorce and the woman who is intentionally building wealth for her daughter's future that distance is not small. That distance is everything.

My daughter asked me once when mommy and daddy were going to get back together.

She was matter of fact about it the way children are matter of fact about the things they want direct, honest, unashamed of the hope behind the question. And I sat down with her and we had one of those conversations that I have come to treasure more than almost anything else in my life. The kind where I talk to her like she is capable of understanding real things. Because she is.

I told her that mommy and daddy love her completely and that is never going to change. And I told her something else something I want her to carry for the rest of her life.

I told her that you do not need another person to be whole. That self love is not something you find in a relationship. It is something you build inside yourself first. And that if she ever chooses to be in a relationship she should go into it as a whole person not a half looking for completion but a whole person choosing to share her wholeness with someone worthy of it.

I told her I was learning that myself. That I was practicing it every day. And that watching me practice it watching me choose myself, set boundaries, wake up with gratitude, build a life I was proud of was the most important thing I could ever teach her.

Some days she makes me cry just by existing. Just by being this joyful, dancing, singing,

resilient little person who wakes up happy every morning the way she has woken up happy every morning since the day she came home from the NICU. She is the reason I started. But she is no longer the only reason I keep going.
I keep going for me too now.
That is new. That is everything.

Kendra Tamika today is a woman who has regained her smile.
Not a performed smile. Not the smile of a woman who is holding herself together and hoping no one looks too closely. The real one. The one that comes from somewhere underneath the surface. The one that people notice without being able to explain exactly what they are noticing they just know something in her is settled. Something in her is at peace. Something in her knows exactly who she is and is not apologizing for any of it.
She regained her joy for life. Her ease. The lightness that gets buried under years of survival mode and quiet suffering and choosing everyone else first.
She looks at her life and she knows not because everything is perfect but because she built it on purpose that she is exactly where she is supposed to be.

Years ago I wanted to believe I could get here without a man. That felt like a radical thought. That felt almost too much to hope for. Because I had been taught by the culture, by the relationships I had watched, by my own long history of making myself smaller in love that a woman needed a man to get certain places in life.

I am here to tell you that is not true.

I got here. Kendra Tamika got here.

With her scripting journal and her morning gratitude and her personal trainer and her no that she says freely and her daughter and her pudding company and her remote job and her sixteen hour drive and her jumping jacks at 1am in a hotel room in a new state.

I got here.

And I want every woman reading this to know that she can too.

Not by following my exact path. By remembering her own power. By doing the internal work. By choosing herself first, consistently, unapologetically, every single day until the life she desires starts to look less like a dream and more like a Tuesday morning.

That is what claiming your power looks like.

Not loud. Not dramatic. Not a single triumphant moment.

Just a woman. Waking up. Saying thank you. Deciding it is going to be a good day.

And meaning it.

Owning Your Power Daily

Claiming your power is not a one time event. It is a practice. And like any practice it requires showing up even on the days it feels uncomfortable especially on those days.

Start with your finances. Not becoming a financial expert overnight just knowing where your money is going. Tracking it. Making one intentional decision this month about how you want it to work for you instead of against you.

Ask yourself the question that changed everything for me: what is the lifestyle I desire? And then figure out what number gets you to the baseline of that life. Start there.

Move your body. Not to punish it. Not to chase a version of yourself from ten years ago. But to honor the body that got you here. The one that carried you through things that should have broken you. That body deserves movement that feels like celebration not punishment.

And protect your no. Practice saying it. Start small if you need to one situation this week where you say no to something that does not feel right in your body. You do not have to explain yourself. You do not have to apologize. No is a complete sentence. And every time you say it honestly you are saying yes to yourself.

The power you have been waiting for is not waiting for a perfect moment. It is waiting for you to decide that right now is enough to begin.

Remember Her Reflection

- What would your mornings look like if you claimed them for yourself before anyone else got access to them?
- What is the no you have been afraid to say and what would it free you to say yes to instead?
- What does the lifestyle you desire actually look like? Have you ever allowed yourself to want it out loud?
- What would it mean to love the body that got you here not the body you used to have or the body you are working toward but this one right now?

Affirmation

You do not need to earn the right to take up space. You do not need to justify your ambition, your desires, or your worth. The woman you have been waiting to become is already standing inside you she has simply been waiting for you to stop asking for permission and start walking.

Remember Her

Power was never something you needed to find. It was something you needed to stop giving away. And the moment you stopped the moment you said no and meant it, the moment you wrote the future before it existed, the moment you looked in the mirror and chose to love what you saw that was the moment you got it back

CHAPTER EIGHT

She Always Had the Power

I was not looking for a calling.

I want to be honest about that because I think there is a version of this story that sounds more poetic than it actually was — the one where a woman in her darkest hour discovers her purpose and everything clicks into place. That is a beautiful story. It is just not mine.

What I was looking for was money.

Specifically I was looking for a way to make money quietly. From home. Without him knowing. While still being present for my daughter because we did not have childcare and I was not going to leave her. I was sitting at my laptop doing what women do when they are trying to figure out how to get from where they are to where they need to be — I was researching. Googling. Following one link to another at whatever hour of the night it was when the house was quiet and my mind was working on the problem of my own survival.

I was not looking for a passion project. I was not looking for a business I would build forever. I was looking for a bridge. Something that would get me from point A to point B. From trapped to free. From no money of my own to enough money to make a plan.

That is how I found the notary business.

And I want to say that clearly because I know some women reading this are waiting for the passion. Waiting for the thing that sets their soul on fire before they take a step. And what I learned in that season is that sometimes the bridge is not the destination. Sometimes you do not need to be passionate about the thing that gets you out. You just need to be willing to build it.

The process of becoming a notary in Texas was not complicated. The exam was open book. I studied. I passed. I got my certification. And then I kept researching because I quickly learned that a basic notary commission alone was not going to generate the kind of income I needed.

That research led me to loan signing. Remote online notarization was taking off at the time and a company called Notarize required their notaries to also be certified loan signing agents. So I went through that process too. More studying. More certification. More quiet deliberate work done in the margins of a life that did not yet know it was about to change.

When it started working I was making around four thousand dollars a month.

I want you to sit with that number for a moment in the context of where I was. A woman who needed to save money in secret. Who did not have childcare. Who was trying to build an exit strategy while living inside the situation she was exiting. Four thousand dollars a month from a laptop at home while my daughter was taken care of and no one knew what I was building.

That money was not just income.

It was proof.

Proof that I could generate something on my own. Proof that my ability to provide for myself and my daughter was not dependent on anyone else's cooperation or permission or presence. Proof that the woman who had spent years believing she needed someone else to make things work was capable had always been capable of making things work entirely on her own.

The notary business was never the dream. But it gave me something more valuable than the dream in that moment.

It gave me the first step.

Rebuilding the pudding company was a different kind of work.

This was not a bridge. This was a reclamation.

When the divorce was finalized everything was turned over to me in the decree. The business. The brand. The recipes. The thing I had created in a friend's kitchen tested and developed and poured myself into was officially, legally, completely mine. Which meant the rebuilding was also completely mine. No partner. No split responsibilities. No one else's vision competing with my own.

Just me. And what I had always known how to do.

I already understood the process from building it the first time so I moved through it with intention. Got my LLC established. Secured the commercial kitchen. Obtained all the permits and licenses required to sell food properly and legally. Sourced the equipment I needed. Did all of it while living at my parents' house, saving money, building the infrastructure of something I was going to do right this time.

And then I went back to the farmers market.
Thursday and Friday mornings I was in the kitchen. Making the jars. Preparing the product. Getting everything ready. Saturday and Sunday I was at the booth. Just me. No team. No help. Completely bootstrapped in the way that the early stages of any real business are bootstrapped you do everything yourself because you are the only one there and the only way forward is through.

The hardest part of that season was not the work. I have never been afraid of work. The hardest part was the aloneness of it. Building something solo after years of believing that the team was what made the thing possible. Learning that actually actually the team had never been the asset.

I was the asset.

And I did not fully understand how true that was until the customers started coming back.

They remembered me. Not the business name. Not the booth. Me. They came back looking for the pudding and when they found it their faces did something I was not prepared for. They lit up. They said they had been waiting. Two years. Three years. They had kept looking for us at the market and we had not been there and they had missed it.

But here is the part that stayed with me.

A lot of those customers did not know I was the one who had created it.

They had seen the business before. They had bought the pudding before. But the face they had seen behind the booth was his because he had been the one selling while I was in the kitchen.

They had fallen in love with a product and never known who made it. Never known whose hands had developed the recipe, whose creative vision had built the brand, whose idea the whole thing had been from the very beginning.

They thought it was him.

I stood there behind that booth and felt the full weight of that realization settle into my body.

For years I had been the invisible engine of something that carried someone else's face. I had been the creator, the developer, the talent and I had stayed so far behind the scenes that the people who loved what I made did not even know I existed.

Not anymore.

I was the face now. I was the brand. I was the person standing in front of the thing I had built and saying without words this came from me. This has always come from me. And I am not stepping back from it ever again.

While I was living at my parents' house building the pudding company back up I was also doing something else quietly.

I was studying.

Project management certifications. Scrum. The credentials that would eventually get me back into a career that could support the life I was trying to build. Not because I had abandoned the pudding company that was always going to be mine, always going to be part of my story but because I understood something practical and important about building financial stability.

You need multiple streams. You need a foundation that is not dependent on the variability of a small business in its rebuilding phase. You need something consistent under you while you grow everything else.

So I studied. I got certified. I built my resume back up. I applied for positions. And in 2023 I landed a remote project management role that paid more than enough.

I want to tell you what that first paycheck felt like.

Not the number the feeling.

It felt like exhaling a breath I had been holding for years. It felt like the ground becoming solid under my feet in a way it had not been solid in longer than I wanted to admit. It felt like being able to look at my daughter and know not hope, not pray, not cross my fingers but know that she was provided for. That her needs were met. That I could give her not just what she needed but what she wanted. That I could start thinking about investing, about building, about creating the kind of financial legacy that changes what is possible for the generation that comes after you.

I was grateful. Deeply, specifically, personally grateful for every person in my support system who had held me up during the years it took to get there. My mother. My family. The friends who showed up. The people who believed in me when I was still figuring out how to believe in myself.

Nobody gets there alone. And I want to say that clearly in a chapter about independence because I think those two things are not opposites. Independence does not mean you did it without any help. It means you did it without giving your power away. It means the help you received lifted you without diminishing you. It means you remained the author of your own story even when other people were in the pages with you.

I had good people in my pages.
And I arrived.
The book that changed how I thought about money was not a finance textbook.
It was called The Richest Man in Babylon.
Someone gave it to me during one of the hardest seasons and I want to pass that gift forward through these pages. It taught me things about financial literacy in the form of ancient parables that somehow landed more clearly than any spreadsheet or budget template ever had. It taught me that wealth is not about how much you make — it is about what you do with what you make. That a portion of everything you earn belongs to you first. That money left to grow will grow. That the habits of financial discipline are available to anyone willing to practice them regardless of where they are starting from.
I wish someone had put that book in my hands twenty years ago.
But I also know that I might not have been ready to receive it twenty years ago. Some lessons arrive exactly when you are prepared to learn them. And what I learned from that book and from everything I lived through is this:
Always put something aside. Not when you have enough. Now. Whatever now looks like. Twenty dollars. Fifty dollars. Whatever you can. Because the habit of saving is more important than the amount. The habit tells your nervous system that you are safe. The habit tells your future self that she was thought of.
Always invest in something that can grow without your constant attention. A product. A skill. A financial instrument. Something that works while you sleep.

Because your time is finite and your energy is finite and the most powerful financial move you can make is creating something that generates value beyond the hours you personally put in.

And always always think five steps ahead.

Not because life cooperates with plans. It often does not. But because the woman who has thought five steps ahead makes better decisions in the present. She is not just reacting. She is building. And there is a profound difference between a woman who is reacting to her financial life and a woman who is building it.

I spent too many years reacting.

I am building now.

And what I know what I want every woman reading this to understand in her bones is that the power to build was never something I acquired. It was never something I was given or taught or rescued into.

It was always mine.

Waiting in the kitchen where I tested pudding recipes late at night. Waiting in the laptop where I researched notary certifications in secret. Waiting in the farmers market booth where customers came back after three years because they had never stopped looking for what I made.

It was always mine.

It has always been yours.

Building What Is Yours

When I got my notary certification nobody threw a party. Nobody called it a breakthrough.

It was a quiet Tuesday and a practical decision but it changed everything because it was mine.

That is what I want you to understand about building your independence. It rarely looks impressive from the outside at first. It looks like studying for a certification nobody asked you to get. It looks like saving money quietly while your life is still uncertain. It looks like showing up to a farmers market with a product you believe in not knowing if anyone will stop at your table.

But every one of those small unglamorous moves is the foundation.

So start where you are. If you have a skill you have been underusing dust it off. If there is a certification that has been sitting in the back of your mind look it up today. If you have a creative gift that someone once made you feel small about return to it. It was always yours.

Learn your numbers. Not because money is everything but because understanding your finances is understanding your options. And options are freedom. Ask yourself the question that changed everything for me: what is the lifestyle I desire? And then figure out what number gets you to the baseline of that life.

And find your version of The Richest Man in Babylon. Find the resource that teaches you to think about money differently. Not as something that happens to you but as something you steward. Not as something you react to but as something you build.

The power was never gone. It was waiting for you to come back and claim it.

Remember Her Reflection

- What skill or resource do you already have that could become a bridge to your next level if you gave it your full attention?
- What is the thing you created the idea, the recipe, the vision that someone else may have been getting credit for? How do you reclaim it?
- What does the lifestyle you desire actually require financially? Have you ever sat down and figured out the number?
- What is one financial habit you could start today no matter how small that your future self would thank you for?

Affirmation

Your resourcefulness is not a backup plan. It is your superpower. Every certification earned, every dollar saved, every idea you brought to life from nothing is proof of something that no one can take from you. You have always had what it takes. The only question was when you were going to remember it.

Remember Her

Independence is not just financial. It is the feeling of standing in your own life and knowing with complete certainty that you built this. Nobody gave it to you. Nobody can take it away. You built it. And you can build more.

CHAPTER NINE

Whole, Not Half

The hardest person I ever had to forgive was myself.

Not him. Not the situation. Not the women who came before me in his life or the friends who tried to tell me or the circumstances that kept me in something longer than I should have stayed. All of that forgiveness came. But it came after. Because before I could forgive anyone else I had to face the one that lived closest the forgiveness that required me to look in the mirror and release the woman who had not known how to love herself sooner.

That was the one that cost the most.

Because forgiving someone else for what they did to you is painful but it has a clear object. There is a person, a behavior, a specific harm that you are releasing. But forgiving yourself for what you did not know for the years you spent accepting less than you deserved because you did not yet understand what you deserved that forgiveness has no clean edges. It asks you to have compassion for a version of yourself that you have already moved past. It asks you to look back at her without contempt.

She did not know what she did not know.

And she deserved grace for that.

I want to tell you what forgiveness actually felt like in my body because I think we talk about it in the abstract too often. We say forgive and move on as if it is a decision you make once on a Tuesday and then it is done. That has not been my experience.

For me forgiveness felt like my shoulders dropping.

Like a breath becoming stable after a long time of shallow breathing. Like teeth I had been clenching releasing. Like a room in my mind that had been occupied cluttered, loud, constantly running suddenly going quiet and creating space for something new.

The shift happened when I stopped asking what was done to me and started asking what I was supposed to learn. That question changed everything. Because it took the person out of the center of the story and put the lesson there instead. It allowed me to look at what I had been through and say — you were a tool. You served a purpose in my story. You taught me things I could not have learned any other way. And now I am releasing you from the role of villain so I can receive the gift of what this cost me.

That does not mean I invited everyone back into my orbit.

Forgiveness and proximity are not the same thing. I forgave people I will never speak to again. I released things that did not require me to maintain a relationship with the person who caused them. Forgiveness is an internal act. It is something you do for the space it creates inside you not for the person who harmed you, not as an invitation for them to return, not as a statement that what happened was acceptable.

It is a reclamation of your own peace.
For her father it was different because he is her father. He will always be her father. And so forgiveness there was not just for me it was for her. For the quality of life she deserves with both of her parents present and functional and not poisoned by the unresolved residue of what her parents went through. She did not ask to be born into our story. She deserved the best version of both of us that we could offer.
So I forgave. For me. And for her.
And every time something comes up in co-parenting that tests that forgiveness and things do come up, they always do I go back to that practice. I take them out of the picture. I ask what I am supposed to learn. I release what I cannot control. And I keep showing up for her because she is always the reason I choose the higher road.

I have non negotiables now.
This is new. Or rather the honoring of them is new. I had instincts before. I had things that felt wrong, things my body responded to with that tightening I described in the last chapter. But I negotiated with those instincts. I explained them away. I told myself I was overreacting or being too demanding or expecting too much.
I do not do that anymore.
In romantic relationships my biggest non negotiable is the unwillingness to respect my boundaries from the very beginning. Not after months of patterns. Not after the relationship is established. From the very beginning.

Because I have learned through years of lived experience that how someone treats your boundaries when they are first establishing themselves with you tells you everything about how they will treat them when the relationship is comfortable and the stakes are higher.

I used to dismiss early boundary violations. I told myself they would learn. That it was just who they were. That I was being rigid. I know better now. The person who does not respect your no when it is easy to respect it will not respect it when it is hard. That is information. Receive it.

In friendships my non negotiable is reciprocity. Not a perfect mathematical equation relationships are not spreadsheets. But effort. The sense that someone is showing up for this the way I am showing up for it. That the care flows in both directions. I have released friendships that I held onto far longer than I should have because I applied the same Good Woman logic to platonic relationships that I applied to romantic ones giving and giving and calling the imbalance loyalty.

It was not loyalty. It was a pattern I had to break.

In family my non negotiable is harder because family carries its own particular weight. But I have gotten significantly better at saying no to things I do not agree with or do not want to do regardless of who is asking. Because the truth is simple and uncomfortable: I have to go to sleep at night inside my own choices. No one else lives in my body. No one else carries the weight of a yes that was not true. I do. And I have decided that my peace my actual daily lived peace is worth protecting even from the people I love.

I walk into every room now like I have ten thousand ancestors walking with me.

I want you to feel that image. Not just read it feel it. The weight of every woman who came before you, every woman who survived something and kept going, every woman whose endurance made your existence possible. When I walk into a space now I carry all of them. I am not just Kendra Tamika from Texas. I am the accumulation of every woman in my lineage who was strong enough to make it to the next day.

That changes how you stand. That changes how you speak. That changes what you are willing to accept in a room.

Operating from wholeness does not mean operating without fear. I want to be clear about that because I think the idea of wholeness can feel impossibly clean like a woman who has arrived at wholeness has somehow transcended the ordinary human experience of uncertainty and doubt. That is not what this is.

Fear is sometimes information. Sometimes the tightening in your chest is not anxiety to be pushed through it is your intuition trying to get your attention. The work is learning to tell the difference between the fear that protects you and the fear that limits you. Between the instinct that is keeping you safe and the old story that is keeping you small.

What I do differently now is I ask. I sit with the fear and I ask is this protecting me or shrinking me? Is this my intuition or my wound? And then I respond to what is actually there instead of reacting to the loudest voice in the room.

I no longer move from a place of needing to be chosen. I move from a place of knowing my worth and waiting for what matches it. I no longer dim myself so that someone else can feel bright. I no longer make myself easier to be around by making myself less of who I am.

I belong in every room I walk into. Not because someone gave me permission. Because I walked in.

If you are still in the middle of it if you are reading this from inside the situation I have been describing, feeling something shift but not yet sure what to do with the shifting I want to speak directly to you.

Push through.

I know that sounds simple. I know it does not capture the complexity of what you are living. But I mean it in the deepest way I know how to mean something. Push through. Not recklessly. Not without a plan. But do not let the weight of where you are convince you that where you are is where you will always be.

Start your day with gratitude. I know that sounds like a bumper sticker. I am telling you it is a practice that will change the chemistry of your days. Before your feet hit the floor. Before you check your phone. Before the day makes its demands on your attention. Say thank you. List five things. Declare that it is going to be a good day. Not because everything is fine because you are choosing to be the source of your own good day instead of waiting for circumstances to create it.

And do the mirror work. Even when it feels ridiculous. Especially when it feels ridiculous. Stand in front of your own reflection and say the things out loud that you need to believe. I am beautiful. I am worthy. I love you. Say them before you believe them. Say them so consistently that one day you realize you stopped performing them and started meaning them.

Because here is what I know from the other side:

One day you are going to look in the mirror and not recognize the woman looking back. Not because she is a stranger. But because she is so fully herself that you had forgotten what fully yourself looked like. And you are going to think there she is. There is the woman I was always supposed to become.

That day is coming. Keep going toward it.

What I believe about love now is different from everything I was taught about it.

I used to believe love was something that happened to you. That it arrived in a feeling butterflies, electricity, the heavens opening up. And I chased that feeling. I mistook intensity for depth, chemistry for compatibility, the inability to walk away for the right reason to stay.

I know better now.

Love is not a feeling that overwhelms you. Love is a decision that reveals itself over time. It is consistent. It is safe. It is the presence of someone who shows up not just on the easy days but on the hard ones, not just when it is convenient but when it costs something.

I watched Michelle Obama talk about this once. She spoke about love not as something that arrives fully formed but as something that develops that the idea of love at first sight is more about attraction than love, and that real love is built in the ordinary moments, the difficult conversations, the choosing of each other when choosing each other is not easy.

That stayed with me.

Because I had spent so much of my life confusing the lightning bolt for the foundation. And lightning bolts are real and they are beautiful but you cannot build a life on a lightning bolt. You build a life on something steadier. Something that is still there when the electricity fades and what remains is just two people deciding every day to choose each other.

My non negotiables now are the foundation of what I will build any future love on.

Not a long superficial list of physical preferences. The core things. The values. The ways of being in the world that I know I need to see consistently over time. The behaviors that tell me someone is safe. The red flags I will no longer negotiate with regardless of how much I like someone in the beginning.

Because the red flags I ignored in the beginning always became the reasons it ended.

That is not a coincidence. That is a pattern. And I am done repeating patterns.

My daughter is neurodivergent.

She moves through the world in her own particular way with a joy and a directness and an unbothered quality that I find myself studying sometimes.

She does not dim herself for rooms. She does not perform comfort for other people's benefit. She shows up fully as who she is with a confidence that is not arrogance it is just the complete absence of the belief that she needs to be different than she is to be acceptable.

She is still becoming. She has her moments of insecurity, especially as she moves toward her teenage years. She asks questions about herself and her place in the world the way all children do. And in those moments I understand that what I say to her matters less than what she watches me do.

She is watching me.

She has always been watching me.

And what I want her to see what I am committed every single day to showing her is a woman who loves herself. Not perfectly. Not without struggle. But consistently and visibly and without apology. A woman who says no when she means no. A woman who walks into rooms with her head up. A woman who built a life she is proud of not because someone handed it to her but because she decided she was worth building it for.

I do not want her to think she needs someone else to complete her. I want her to understand that she is already whole that if love comes into her life it should come as a complement to her wholeness not a solution to her emptiness.

She taught me that by being exactly who she is.

Unapologetically. Joyfully. Completely.

She wakes up happy every single morning.

And some days I look at her and I think that is what it looks like to be whole. Right there. That is the whole point.

You are not a half.

I need you to hear that clearly and let it settle somewhere deep before you turn the page. You are not a half waiting to be completed. You are not a work in progress who needs to be finished before you are worthy of love. You are not a healing woman who needs to become a healed woman before your life can really begin.

You are whole right now.

In this season. In this body. With this history and these wounds and these lessons still being learned. You are whole. The relationships you enter from this place will be different from every relationship you have ever been in before. Not because you found the right person because you became the right person. For yourself first. And when a whole woman chooses love she chooses it from abundance not from scarcity. From fullness not from need. From the clear-eyed knowledge of what she deserves and the patience to wait for what matches it.

That is not loneliness. That is power.

That is what whole looks like.

Living Your Transformation

Transformation asks very little of you all at once. It only ever asks for the next right step.

Set your boundaries and say them out loud. Not aggressively. Not apologetically. Just clearly. Decide what you will accept and what you will not and then let your actions match that decision. Your non negotiables are not a wish list. They are a declaration of what you value about yourself.

Write things down. Journal it. Script it. Write the version of your future you are too afraid to say out loud yet and read it back to yourself until it stops feeling like fantasy and starts feeling like a plan.

Forgive yourself. Specifically and genuinely. For not knowing sooner. For staying longer than you should have. For loving people who were not yet capable of loving you back in the way you needed. You were doing the best you could with what you knew. You know more now. That is enough.

And do the mirror work. Every day. Especially on the days it feels impossible. Stand there and say the words. Put the armor on. Because one day sooner than you think you are going to look up and not be able to tell where the armor ends and the real you begins.

Because they will have become the same thing.

Remember Her Reflection

- What is the one thing you need to forgive yourself for that you have been carrying the longest?
- What are your actual non negotiables not the ones you think you should have but the ones your body already knows?
- What would it feel like to walk into every room like you have ten thousand ancestors walking with you?
- What do you want the young women watching you to learn from how you love yourself?

Affirmation

You do not need to be finished healing to be worthy of love. You do not need to be perfect to deserve respect. You are whole right now in this moment, in this season, exactly as you are. Transformation is not a destination. It is a direction. And you are already moving.

Remember Her

You were never a half searching for completion. You were always a whole learning to believe it. And the moment you stopped looking for someone to complete you and started completing yourself was the moment everything changed.

CHAPTER TEN

The Woman in the Mirror

I want to go back to the beginning.

Not to relive it. Not to change it. But to do the one thing I could not do when I was inside it I want to sit across from the woman in that hospital bed and look her directly in the eyes and say the thing she needed to hear most.

I can see her so clearly.

She is lying in a room with grayish green walls and a window that shows her nothing but sky when the sun is out. There are machines beside her. A belly band monitoring the baby she is fighting to keep alive. Thrombosis wraps around her legs. The television is on but she is not really watching it. She is doing what she has always done holding everything together on the inside while appearing composed on the outside.

And the man she loves is sitting right there in the room with her asking her a question she does not want to answer.

I want to sit down beside her. I want to take her hand. And I want to look her in the eyes and say the two words that would have changed everything if she had believed them in that moment.

Speak your truth.

Not carefully. Not strategically. Not after calculating the consequences or considering his feelings or worrying about what it will mean for the children or the relationship or the image of the good woman she has been working so hard to maintain.

Just speak it.

Whatever happens after is what happens after. But at least she will not be carrying it. At least she will not be lying in that hospital bed with machines tracking her vital signs and a truth sitting in her chest getting heavier by the hour a truth she is already paying a physical price to suppress.

Speak your truth.

I replay that moment sometimes. Even now. It is one of the moments I carried the longest the resentment of it, directed at him and at myself in equal measure. At him for asking. At myself for answering the way I did. And what I know now, from the distance of everything that came after, is that the resentment was not really about the trip to California.

It was about all the times before that I had not spoken. All the truths I had swallowed. All the moments I had chosen his comfort over my own honesty until the habit of silence became so ingrained that I did it automatically reflexively, without even deciding to anymore.

If I could give that woman one thing it would not be a warning. It would not be a preview of everything that was coming. It would be permission. Permission to open her mouth and say what was true. Permission to take up the space her feelings deserved. Permission to be, in that moment, something other than accommodating.

She already had everything she needed.
She just needed permission to use it.

What I know now that I wish I had known then is this:
I am her.
Not the version of her that the world tried to define. Not the version that the Good Woman rules tried to contain. Not the version that stayed quiet in hospital beds and swallowed truths and chose everyone else's peace over her own.
The real her.
The one who is a goddess in her own right. The one whose words speak life into everything she touches. The one who understands finally, completely, without reservation that she is a creator. That women are creators. That we carry life inside our bodies and birth entire worlds into existence and there is no force on this earth more powerful than a woman who has remembered what she is.
I know now how powerful my thoughts are. How powerful my words are. That what I speak over myself and over my life does not disappear into the air it lands. It takes root. It becomes. The scripting I did in those early morning hours before the world woke up was not wishful thinking. It was architecture. I was building the life I wanted to live one written sentence at a time, one spoken declaration at a time, one morning of gratitude at a time.
I know now that I can have anything I desire in this world.
Not because the universe owes it to me. Not because the path will be easy or the timing will be convenient or the obstacles will politely step aside.

But because I am willing to do the internal work that makes external results possible. Because I have learned that the life I want begins with the woman I decide to be and I have decided.

I decided a long time ago, actually.

In a hospital room with grayish green walls.

I just did not know it yet.

The other day I was doing my mirror work.

Standing in front of my reflection the way I have learned to stand not rushing past it, not doing the quick glance and moving on, but actually stopping. Actually looking. Actually being present with the woman looking back at me.

And I saw something I want to try to describe.

I saw light.

Not a metaphor something I actually perceived when I looked at my own face. A light that was not there before. Not the performance of happiness, not the smile I used to wear as a mask to make everyone around me comfortable. Something underneath all of that. Something that does not require anyone else's presence or validation or acknowledgment to exist.

It is unapologetic that light. It is matter of fact. It does not ask for permission or explain itself or make itself smaller so the room does not feel crowded. It just is. Steady and warm and completely at home in the face it is living in.

I looked at that woman and I thought there she is. There is the woman I have been becoming. There is the woman who drove sixteen hours with a toothache and tears on her face and did not turn around.

There is the woman who did jumping jacks in a hotel room at one in the morning because she had come too far to not wake up for what was waiting on the other side. There is the woman who rebuilt a business from a friend's kitchen and stood at a farmers market booth and let people see her really see her for the first time.

There is the woman who remembered herself.

She is filled with love. She is filled with joy. She carries both of those things not because her life is perfect or her journey is finished or she has arrived at some final destination where nothing hard can reach her anymore. She carries them because she has learned through everything it took to learn it that love and joy are not things that happen to you. They are things you decide.

Every morning when you open your eyes and say thank you.

Every time you say no and mean it.

Every time you look in the mirror and choose to see something worthy of love looking back.

My prayer for you the woman holding this book is simple.

I want you to feel seen.

Not the seen of being observed or studied or analyzed. The seen of being known. The seen of reading a page and thinking she is talking about me. She knows what this feels like. I am not alone in this. Someone has been where I am and came out the other side and is standing here telling me it is possible.

You are not alone in this.
Whatever version of this story you are living whether you are in the hospital bed or the NICU months or the wandering years or the first night on the apartment floor or somewhere in between all of it you are not alone. The details of my story are mine. But the feeling underneath them the quiet erosion of self, the weight of carrying everything, the long slow journey back to who you were before the world told you who to be that feeling belongs to so many of us.
And I want you to know that it does not have to be where you stay.
I want you to close this book and feel that reclaiming your power is not a fantasy for other women. It is not reserved for the women who had easier starting points or better circumstances or more support or fewer obstacles. It is available to you. Right now. In the life you are already living. With the resources you already have. Starting with the one thing no one can take from you your decision to remember who you are.
I want you to feel enough.
Not almost enough. Not enough if you just fixed this thing or healed that wound or became a better version of yourself first. Enough right now. Worthy right now. Powerful right now. In this body in this season with this history and these scars and these lessons still being learned.
You are enough.
You have always been enough.
You are that girl.

Here is what I am certain of.
I have the right to be here.
Not in the apologetic way not in the way of someone who has been given permission by external forces and is grateful for the allowance. In the declarative way. The way of a woman who has looked at her own life clearly all of it, every hard chapter, every moment she wishes she had done differently, every season that cost her more than it should have and arrived at the unshakeable conclusion that none of it diminished her right to take up space in this world.
I belong in every room I walk into.
I am worthy of every conversation I participate in, every dream I pursue, every good thing I allow myself to receive. The love I spent years searching for in other people I found it. It was inside me the whole time. It was waiting in the mirror. It was waiting in the morning gratitude. It was waiting in every no I was too afraid to say and every truth I was too afraid to speak.
I only surround myself with that love now.
Not perfectly. Not without the daily practice of choosing it again and again. But intentionally. Consistently. As a non negotiable truth about how I move through the world.
My words speak life.
My presence matters.
My story this story, the one you just read, the one that started in a hospital bed with a woman saying yes when she meant no this story was always moving toward something. Not in spite of the hard parts. Because of them. Every breaking point was a building point in disguise. Every season of wandering was a season of becoming. Every moment I lost myself was a moment that eventually, inevitably, led me back to her.

So, here is what I want to leave you with.

Not a list. Not a final set of action steps. Just this.

There is a woman inside you who has been waiting.

She has been waiting through the relationships that asked too much of you and gave too little back. Through the seasons of survival where you carried everything alone. Through the quiet erosions and the loud breakdowns and all the ordinary Tuesday mornings where you showed up for everyone else and forgot to show up for yourself.

She has been patient with you.

She has never left.

And she does not need you to be finished healing or fully rebuilt or completely certain before she welcomes you back. She just needs you to turn toward her. To stop moving away from her in the direction of everyone else's needs and start moving toward her. One morning. One no. One truth spoken out loud. One moment of standing in front of your mirror and choosing to see something worthy of love looking back.

That is how it starts.

Not with a dramatic transformation. Not with a perfect plan. With a turning. A choosing. A remembering.

So I am going to ask you to do something before you close this book.

Find a mirror.

Stand in front of it. Really stand there. And look at the woman looking back at you not quickly, not critically, not with the running commentary of everything you wish were different. Just look at her.

And then say this out loud. In your own voice. To your own face.

I see you. I love you. I honor all that you are and all that you are still becoming.

Say it before you believe it. Say it especially before you believe it. And keep saying it every morning, every hard day, every moment the old voice rises up with its old stories about who you are and what you deserve and how much space you are allowed to take up.

Keep saying it until the day you realize you mean it completely.

Because that day is coming.

She is coming.

She has actually been here all along.

Remember her.

And when you remember her, be her.

And never forget her.

Remember Her Reflection

- If you could sit across from the youngest version of yourself the one who first learned to shrink what would you say to her?
- What truth have you been carrying in silence that deserves to finally be spoken out loud?
- What does the woman in your mirror look like when you really stop and look? What do you see that you have been moving past too quickly?
- What is the one thing you are going to do differently starting today not someday, not when the time is right, but today to begin remembering her?

Affirmation

This is not the end of the book. This is the beginning of the life you were always meant to live. Every page you read was a step back toward yourself. Every reflection was an act of courage. Every truth you sat with was a declaration that you matter that your story matters that she matters. Now go live like you know it.

Remember Her

You have always been the woman you were waiting for.
Now go be her. Fully. Unapologetically. Without permission. Without apology. Without ever dimming that light again.
The world needs you fully.
Not the version of you that keeps the peace at the cost of herself.
Not the version that says yes when she means no.
Not the version that carries everything alone and calls it strength.
The full version.
The real one.
The one who just remembered who she is.

Remember her.
And when you remember her, be her.
And never, ever forget her again.

Go Be Her.

As you close this book, remember: the power you seek has always been within you.
Take a deep breath, look in the mirror, and remember her.
Your full, unapologetic, unshakable self.
Not the version of you that keeps the peace at the cost of herself. Not the version that says yes when she means no.
Not the version that carries everything alone and calls it strength.
The full version. The real one. The one who just remembered who she is.
Let today be the first of many days you honor your worth, your joy, and your life fully.
And when you look in that mirror — really look — say it out loud one more time.
I see you. I love you. I honor all that you are and all that you are still becoming.
She has been waiting for you.
Go be her.

To every woman who

This book would not exist without the people who held me when I had nothing left to hold myself with.

To my mother — you were my rock in the hospital, in the NICU, in every season where I needed someone who would come without being asked. Thank you for showing up every single time. I love you more than these words can carry.

To my daughter — you are the reason this story exists and the reason it matters. You came into this world fighting and you have never stopped. Watching you grow into the joyful, brilliant, unbothered person you are becoming is the greatest privilege of my life. Every boundary I set, every truth I spoke, every morning I chose to get up and keep going — it was all for you. And it was all worth it. This book is for you. Everything is for you.

To my family — for the dinners at mom's house when the apartment felt too quiet, for the aunties who showed up, for the grandparents who gave my daughter community when I could not give her everything I wanted to. For the support that asked nothing in return and gave everything anyway. You are my foundation. You always have been.

To the friends who tried to tell me the truth before I was ready to hear it — I see you now. I hear you now. Thank you for loving me enough to say the hard thing even when I was not ready to receive it. You were right. You were always right. And I am grateful you stayed anyway.

To every woman who sat beside me, encouraged me, celebrated me, and reminded me of who I was during the seasons when I had completely forgotten — this book carries your energy on every single page.

To the therapist who looked at me and said: I do not even see you in this relationship — thank you. That sentence changed everything. Sometimes the most powerful thing someone can do for you is tell you the truth clearly enough that you cannot un-hear it.

And to every woman who picks up this book in her hardest season — the one who is lying in a hospital bed saying yes when she means no, the one who is on the floor of a hallway falling apart, the one who is sitting on an air mattress in an empty apartment wondering if she made the right decision, the one who is driving sixteen hours toward a life she built on purpose and crying behind the wheel and keeping going anyway —

This was written for you.

You are seen. You are enough. You are that girl.

Now go remember her.

www.ingramcontent.com/pod-product-compliance
Lightning Source LLC
LaVergne TN
LVHW090530110826
845146LV00003B/1047

* 9 7 9 8 9 9 5 4 7 0 5 0 2 *